Come Talk with Me

Sara Jane Briggs

Published by Argyle Fox Publishing, argylefoxpublishing.com

Publisher holds no responsibility for content of this work. Content is the sole responsibility of the author.

ISBN 979-8-89124-090-2 (Paperback)

ARGYLE FOX
PUBLISHING

My heart has heard you say, "Come and talk with me."
And my heart responds, "Lord, I am coming."

—*Psalm 27:8*

Dedication

To my Heavenly Father, who always welcomes me to come, sit, and talk with Him. Thank You for these lessons and the many more yet to come. Your Word is the very air I breathe.

To Larry Briggs, my husband of fifty-two years, my best friend, my greatest love and partner in ministry. Thank you for always encouraging and cheering me on in every aspect of life.

To Jane Lanham, thank you for reading every lesson and offering advice. Together we laughed at some and deeply sighed at others. I value everything about our friendship.

To Mary Jo Jones, my sister and creator of Jane's Secret Prayer Garden. As God would have it, the garden didn't remain a secret but a place of prayer for many who are broken and in need of healing.

To my siblings, who are my best friends: Ruth Helms, Mary Jo Jones, Jean Nelson, Russell McCarter, Eric McCarter, and Linda Norris. Our lives are as beautifully blended as the stately trees whose branches embrace the country road we all call home.

To Daniel Brantley, my wise, talented, and comical editor and publisher. Thank you for allowing me to call you my favorite son. It confuses people, and that in itself is rewarding!

To Katy McCarter, my niece and owner of Joifulscene Photography. Thank you for the picture of our country road and my dad's workshop. They both make my heart smile, while bringing a tear to my eyes. Priceless.

Table of Contents

Foreword

Our son invited us to Destination Church, and we fell in love with all aspects of the church. Later, God divinely connected Jane Briggs and me during a time of great difficulty. Both Jane's husband and my sister had been diagnosed with life-threatening diseases. Jane and I both served as caregivers for our loved ones. The trauma bonded us in a unique way. Our conversations at church were mainly short phrases: "How are you? Do you need anything? I'm praying for you." There were no phone calls or text messages, but there was an unspoken sense of assurance that we had each other's back.

Then, my life changed again on December 6, 2019. That day I was diagnosed with ductal carcinoma in situ (DCIS), ER/PR positive, Stage 0, Grade 3, and negative for BRCA 1 and 2 gene mutation. This meant my cancer was localized in the ducts, hormones were feeding it, no gene mutation caused it, and it was growing at a rapid rate. I'd fought nearly two decades for this diagnosis. Finally, a medical team confirmed the disease I knew I had but never wanted.

Everything happened quickly, and complications left me flat. During treatment, many reached out to share that they were praying for me. Jane even stopped me at church a couple of times to provide words of comfort. Yet no one understood the physical and mental anguish associated with this dreaded diagnosis. I didn't blame anyone for my feelings. I never wanted anyone else to feel this pain as I asked God what He wanted me to do with this.

Eventually, I joined a support group with other women who understand the trauma associated with the words "You have breast cancer." Here for The Girls, Inc. provides women with various diagnoses and treatment plans a place to feel understood and heard. These women became my safe place.

However, after a New York photoshoot for a feature in *Women's Health* magazine, I realized a few things as while examining my scars in the mirror:

1. Our mental and physical scars speak a story that can heal the wounds of another.
2. Everyone would not join a support group.
3. I had to create a platform for all genders, caregivers, and professionals to share their scars' stories.

The Holy Spirit placed an urgency in my spirit to ensure voices were heard, people knew how to advocate, and I assisted those who don't know how to advocate. This moment catapulted the birthing of the podcast "Our Scars Speak." It's a safe place where people share their testimonies of life before breast cancer, during treatment, and now. No one leaves without a message from God to encourage them along their journey.

Unbeknown to me, Jane was watching from afar. Once again, our paths crossed in a more profound, unexpected way. During a meeting at our spot, Panera, my friend's face lacked its strength and beauty. In its place was an indescribable sadness. My heart dropped when she shared the findings of her mammogram.

She was engulfed in unwavering faith, but the thought of telling her children caused Jane deep pain. Jane had no control over the situation. She had to rely on God and those who He allowed to assist her through her breast cancer journey.

This book provides insight into a woman of God's heart as our Lord molds her heart through the discovery and treatment of a life-threatening disease. Jane's vulnerability takes us inside her ever-growing relationship with Christ. She shows us that a new dimension in Christ can bring us new levels of attacks, but His blood still holds power. She takes the reader into the depths of her emotions that led to exploration of our Father's faithfulness, love, grace, assurance, and mercy.

May each of you be encouraged with this book. I pray everyone feels the love of our sister, Jane, but most of all, the love of the Holy Trinity. Allow your hearts to be open, filled, and transformed as Jane takes you into her war room of lamenting, worship, thanksgiving, and praise.

I am so proud of you, my sister/friend Jane. Remember to take one second at a time as you extend yourself grace. I love you!

Blessings and love,

Christina Miner

Introduction

I stand amazed that God extends a warm invitation to come and talk with Him. He desires to have a heart-to-heart conversation. Come and you'll find, as I did, it's not awkward or uncomfortable. It's not "I know what you did and I'm going to let you have it" time. That's not our Father's heart. Instead, you'll cherish every word shared. You'll yearn for more and more. King David was a man after God's own heart. The reverse is also true. God chases after our hearts. Incredibly, His heart longs to hear from you and me.

Please, come sit with me, as I share a few heart-to-heart conversations I've had with the Father. I trust they will draw you into more time spent talking with Him. Perhaps as we sit together, we'll learn from each other at the feet of Jesus, the One who calls us friends. So come with me. Let our hearts respond, "Lord, I am coming."

As we begin, allow me to share, as friends do, a little about me.

I grew up in a small town in South Carolina. Most of my high school friends still live in the area. Many married high school sweethearts and live the life I expected to live. Even today, my hometown remains basically unchanged. I think it's because those same kind, family-oriented people continue to call it home.

I chose to attend college in Florida, yet planned to return to my cozy town to build my family life. While attending college, I made every effort to visit my family as often as possible. They live outside of town limits in a small community called Bethany. (Don't you just love that name?) There were a few small farms, but like our family, most raised crops to provide for their own families and to share with neighbors. Of course, the only homes nearby were relatives. The acreage belonged to my grandfather who gave land to his children, who gave it to their children. They all built their homes along the winding, dirt country road. Oh, the stories left untold on that red clay pathway! The road is now paved with a yellow line down the middle as family and neighbors have blended as one.

As you turn onto our road, one edge of the asphalt meanders, gently touching the North Carolina lines of Kings Mountain State Park. Beautiful trees with hanging branches welcome you like waving palm branches. Every season is breathtaking, but fall brings a burst of every autumn hue imaginable.

Our community had an old country store where men sat around a potbelly stove in the winter and played checkers. Their stories consisted of fishing and old wives' tales. It seems to me, as a small child, that when fish were caught, they somehow grew two or three times larger once taken from the hook. The merchandise consisted of everything from nails to clothes to farming supplies to penny candy. The only thing I might need to explain is penny candy. For the sake of time, Google it. I could stop and buy gas for the car, grab a coke and a package of peanuts and say, "Daddy will come by later to pay. Just put it on his tab." I knew to never take advantage of my dad, but it was the norm of the day. The family-owned store was built in 1888 and remains today. Oh, how I always wanted to move back! But I never did.

When I'd come home for college breaks, my arrival was recorded in the town's newspaper. I think the paper published once a week—twice if needed. Trust me, I'm nobody special, but they always mentioned when I was home visiting family and stated I would soon return to my college campus in Florida. I often wondered if locals thought I ran away from home or was on the run from college. I'm suspect I always came home on a slow news week or perhaps nothing was on sale at our local grocery store, Community Cash. The store is still open and serving the community as a Piggly Wiggly. Like I said, very little has changed, which brings a comforting smile to my heart. My six siblings remain in the area, loving their children and now grandchildren and a few great-grandchildren. Over these past fifty-three married years, I remain an occasional visitor. God's call on my life became my heart's desire, which took me away from that home, sweet home. I have no regrets, but I stand in awe that He chose a simple country girl from Bethany, South Carolina, to share His Good News.

While I don't live in Bethany any longer, I'm not left out. I'm included in our monthly graduating class email, as they set up lunch meetings with fellow classmates. It's a 350-mile drive for me, so I can't go, but I love seeing the names of my former classmates and remembering the kind, fun times we had together. I've known some of them since first grade. My best friend from high school and I still stay in contact. We met in junior high (now called middle school, an interior term if you ask me), and we haven't seen each other for years. When we call, the conversation picks up as if we just had lunch together. We currently live states apart, but our hearts are woven together. We've laughed, cried, seen great miracles, and experienced incredible heartbreaks. That's why I cherish the gift of friends. They help celebrate the good times and carry us through the difficult seasons of life.

Friends are marvelous gifts God places in our lives. I have some amazing friends. I've also lost relationships with some wonderful people. I've learned the hard way that friends, as valuable as they are, come and go. They are not my entire story. They are chapters in my life and not the whole book. I'm a chapter in the lives of some former friends as well. I hope it's a chapter well read, but I'm rather sure lots of editing had to be done. But that junior high school friendship remains strong as ever. I love you, Diane. You're a friend who is written into every chapter of my story. When you read the lesson on friendship, I trust you see how deeply you are cherished still.

It may be hard to believe, but I'm an extremely private person. Sharing these lessons is like inviting strangers and friends to view a part of me that I never intended to be made public. Yet, God has shown me that the issues I've faced are not uniquely mine; therefore, His mercy and grace that He has poured out over me are not mine to keep. They ought to be shared openly and honestly.

As you read, you'll see the *not-so-good* parts of my walk with Him. I have failed, been bruised and wounded only to get up and try it again. You'd think after almost sixty years of being a Christian I'd be further along, but I know where I started. Without Him, I'd still be at the starting point—or perhaps a few steps backward. So, welcome to my secret battles and how God forgives and picks me up, brushes off my dirty, bruised knees, and sends me on my way. The heavenly kiss from the Father heals even the deepest wounds as He pours fresh oil, grace, and mercy into every morning and wound. My prayer is that at least one of these devotions speaks to you and lifts you back into His arms, brushes you off, and sends you into the next chapter of your journey.

Those who have read my book, *The Long Goodbye*, or viewed our story on The 700 Club ("A Wife's Long Goodbye") have often asked when I would publish my next book? My answer is the same. "I didn't mean to write the first one, so there won't be a second." Then I began to write in the same manner—to record good and hard times and how God walked me into and through paths I'd never survive without Him.

I began to record those lessons as the Master Architect put

me under construction. Some walls were built, some made stronger, others torn down completely. Here I am at the golden age of seventy-three, and He's still working on me. Thankfully, He never stops working, and His construction will continue until my last breath. That's a good thing. I have so many areas that need to be chipped away, burned into ashes, and made beautiful again.

One person who hasn't stopped asking me to write another book is our friend Ron. He is a great chapter in the lives of many people. He asked me to write about our life in the ministry for the past fifty-three years. I'd do that, but I'd have to put it in the fiction section as only a few would believe it. Honestly, my husband and I don't realize our journey isn't normal until we share stories with others. When we do, people listen with eyes wide. Some become scared or laugh their heads off. Larry and I glance at each other, silently wondering what just happened.

A few years ago, I was asked to share at a Ladies' Night Out. The topic was aging and adjusting in ministry as I've aged. I made serious, thoughtful notes composed of conflicts and victories in marriage and ministry. Then, I went over my allotted time. As I spoke, people responded in laughter. I repeated a few sentences—not to get a response, but to make sure I said what I meant to say, which was not meant to be funny at all. With each repeat the laughter grew. I realized what I thought was very normal must have not been!

My life consists of events I think have no real impact on others' lives until I see and hear their reactions. As I said, I never planned to live outside my little town, but then entered the call of God. Each day, He smiles and says, "You don't have a clue how I love using simple, ordinary, everyday people to do extraordinary things for Me." I don't believe I'm doing anything extraordinary, but God's heart smiles when He sees I'm willing to try.

Perhaps you and I will become friends as you turn each page. I'd be honored. So, sit back. Take your time. Get a cup of coffee and a comfy blanket, and let's see what God has planned as we begin lessons from *Come Talk with Me*.

—Sara Jane Briggs

Lessons from a Grandchild

If this isn't about me, then who is this about?

Tunnel Vision: Ability to see a situation from one angle, neglecting or ignoring other important possibilities.

What if life events, whether wonderful blessings or terrible heartbreaks, aren't about you, but about shining a light of praise so brightly that it sets others free?

Maybe it's not about you nor me!

I took my four-year-old granddaughter, Trinity, to the mall to buy her a pair of new shoes. As her mom and I chatted away, Trinity kept interrupting to ask when she'd get her new shoes. Her mom didn't answer her but gently held her hand and kept walking and talking with me.

After several attempts, Trinity stopped in her tracks. She looked up at her mom and asked once again, "When am I getting my shoes?" Her mom looked at her and said, "Trinity, not everything's about you." Sweet Trin says, "I don't get it. Then who is this about?"

She wasn't upset or being rude. In her childlike trust, she wanted assurance that her mom knew she was there and remembered her need. She didn't understand why her shoe plans were taking so long and none of the discussion was about her or her shoes. She never asked again, but the look of disappointment and confusion caused us to focus on finding those shoes.

I secretly tucked that moment into my heart.

How often have I walked beside God asking, "How long is this going to take before I receive what You've said is mine? Are You listening? Is this ever going to happen?"

When heartbreaking moments come with seemingly no

positive end results, I've looked up to the One holding my hand. Like young Trinity, I've asked, "Who is this about if not me? Is it possible that it's for the benefit of someone else?"

Acts 16: 22–40 records one of the many beatings of the Apostle Paul and his coworker Silas. After being thrown into prison, at midnight they were singing hymns of praise to God when an earthquake shook the very foundations of the prison. At once, all the prison doors opened and everyone's chains unfastened. I imagine the sound was deafening as metal doors slammed against stone walls and iron chains crashed to the ground. And what sounds of shock must have come from their lips!

Before the miracle, back up a few verses to the suffering they endured. They were beaten with rods and thrown into the inner prison (dungeon), where their feet were fastened in an agonizing position in the stocks. Their bloody, open wounds pressed against filthy, jagged stone walls. In the midst of this, they didn't look at the Father and say, "You see our situation and what brought us here. Where are You? We need Your help."

They understood their situation wasn't about themselves. It was about lifting Jesus higher so all men would be drawn to Him. God was more than aware of their pain, yet this was about others.

Paul and Silas knew they were physically bound but spiritually free, while the guard who walked about freely was spiritually chained to the walls of sin. Some of the most powerful words I've ever read came next: But about midnight. In the darkest hour, at the height of pain, they prayed and sang hymns of praise.

We aren't told the words of those prayers, but they caused everyone to listen. Those words would not have been about the suffering of Paul and Silas. The other prisoners wouldn't have cared. Such words were common there. After all, other prisoners endured beatings, experienced open wounds, and made their own cries for help in the musty, filthy jail.

The inner dungeon had no light except for the torches used by guards to make sure prisoners were bound tightly in their chains. So, they weren't compassionately moved by the sight of someone else's beatings. This was different. This was praise—praise so powerful it set them all free. Best of all, the jailer—the only one not bound by chains, realized he needed to be freed. As a result, the jailer and his entire family were set free because of the praise that rose from the dark, painful experience of Paul and Silas.

How's that for being free indeed?

Prayer: *Lord, grant me wisdom to understand whether in the simplest disappointments or the depths of despair, this isn't about me. It's about praising You. All attention, all glory, and all honor shines solely on You. I may not see the purpose or understand how you're working it all for good, but I choose to sing your praises until the earth quakes and the chains fall off and we are all free.*

If this isn't about you and me, then who is this about? It's about Him and how He can use our wounds to set others free, as we raise a song of praise in our darkest hour. Yes, while still in chains, still bleeding, still in the cold and dark dungeon, still in the agonizing position, we're called to lift our prayers and sing for those bound in darkness to come to Jesus, bringing along their entire household.

Lessons from a Sinking Ship

Don't Lose Hope

Shipwrecked: To destroy or badly damage something; irretrievable loss or failure.

Are you in a storm against your will? It happens to me often, when I allow the actions of others to crash over me. I've even caused the waves by allowing my thoughts to blow my sails in the wrong direction. Unexpected storms can easily blow us off course. What seems a gentle southern breeze can abruptly worsen into a hurricane force that blows us off course and out to sea.

I encourage you to take the time to read the entire chapter of Act 27. However, for this purpose, I'll share a part of verse 20: "All hope of ever getting through it alive was abandoned."

We can lose lots of things in the midst of storms, but losing hope is the worst. It's like the old pirate movies in which the captive has his hands bound behind him while forced to walk the plank. The captive is bound and outnumbered. That's the picture of verse 20: "All hope of ever getting through it alive was abandoned."

Paul was on a ship with seasoned sailors, but they lost hope of surviving. Losing all hope will shipwreck our lives. Like the others, Paul was afraid, but someone had to step up, believe, and announce the promises of God. In this case, it was Paul. A simple tent maker, he was the only one who wasn't a seasoned sailor, but he knew to put all hope in God. God then encouraged Paul in a vision, which led Paul to champion the entire crew to hope.

I pray that if you're on a sinking ship and expect a shipwreck, you have someone who will stand up, speak up, and bring the encouragement you need. If there isn't such a person, take this life jacket from Jude 1: 20–21: "But you, my delightfully loved friends, constantly and progressively build yourselves up on the foundation of your most holy faith by praying every moment in the Spirit. Fasten your hearts to the love of God (your life jacket) and receive the mercy of our Lord Jesus Christ, who gives us eternal life."

Before you turn the page or move on with your day, may I be your friend of encouragement and pray over you?

Prayer: *Father, thank You for hearing our cry. Our weeping came right into Your heart, and You turned Your face to rescue us. You never slumber nor sleep. Your eye of loving compassion searches the storm, finding us in the raging waves. When we can't seem to find our way back on course, we are never out of your sight. Your word declares You will never leave us abandoned. You will not loosen your grip on our lives. The Lord is for us. We will not fear nor dread. We thought all hope was gone, but You, my Living Hope, have caused the sea to part and to roll back the grip it had on me. You are the Waymaker, opening paths that only You could open. You have become my Power, my Bedrock beneath my feet. You are my Forever Fortress, my Hiding Place and Pathway of Escape. You are my High Tower where the storms cannot reach me. You are my forever Champion.*
I pray for my friend reading this prayer, that You, O Lord, will protect. That You will cast off every heavy weight causing the ship to sink. Replace the burdensome weight with the knowledge that God is Captain of the Ship. You

provide escape to the safety of shore. You will not fail or forsake. In this truth, I pray the reader will not fear but will stand firm on the bow of the ship, proclaiming "God is on my side!"

Don't abandon ship! Stay the course!

Lessons from Friendships

Chapters with Opposite Views

Friends: Trust between two people.

Chapters: A period of time in a person's life.

I consider my friends like chapters in a book. They each have written meaning into my life's story. Research confirms most people have about seven close friends. They are part of your story written over an extended period of time.

Some friends may be totally opposites in personalities, likes and dislikes. If so, is this a good thing? I think when the right combination of opposites attract, it's like finding the missing piece of a puzzle that snaps in place to make the picture reveal its meaning. Polar opposite, however, might be a messy sight. Two extroverts would overwhelm us all. Two introverts may not overwhelm anyone, as we wouldn't know who they are.

One of my very best opposite friends is adventurous. I pretend to be up for adventure, until the adventure begins. She's spontaneous. I keep a checklist to make sure we've planned well in advance. She rescues dogs, and I babysit my children's dogs on occasion. (Let's be honest. I dogsit often.) Her personality is a chihuahua. Mine is a toy poodle. She leads, and I follow, nipping at her heels and asking, "What on earth are we doing?" When we greet people, she nods her hello, while I run and hug them.

Before she deserted me by moving to Maine, we both lived here in Virginia. Our favorite summer trip was going to Virginia Beach. We did it often, and we never went or returned the same way. If I had to guess, I'd say we got lost 100 percent of the time. She'd say we just took a different route. No matter what, we laughed until we could barely breathe.

One thing we have in common is our first name, Jane. To make it clear, I determined she's Jane One and I'm Jane Two. Makes sense to me. When I mention her, I always say, "My friend Jane in Maine." She is definitely a chapter in my book of life. The subtitle would read: "Trust between two people."

She moved to Maine for the beautiful scenery captured in the fall, along with Maine's crisp autumn air. My favorite season is spring, when everything comes to life. I also appreciate the first few weeks of fall—cool mornings with warm afternoons. Fall foliage is a beauty to behold. However, when the leaves fall to the ground, I feel a little down, too.

Why do trees drop their leaves? I understand the scientific reasons, but it doesn't seem to make it easier. Those barren limbs seem so silent and lonely. Yet, I appreciate the reason. It's a preamble to spring, a necessity to make room for new life. The old is not wasted. The leaves cover the soil like a warming blanket, fertilizing and preparing new life to begin afresh. Without fall there would be no spring. Without my opposite friend, I would be a rather dull spring.

Are you in a season of your life that isn't your favorite? Take heart. This season has a purpose. It may seem your opposite season, but it has a purpose greater than your current happiness. It covers you and prepares you for the new life plans God has for you. His thoughts are for peace and not anxiousness, for a future and a hope. It's not to harm you but to bless you.

Do you see these opposites? Therefore, don't dread it. Don't rush through it. Don't view this season as barren and cold and lifeless. It's okay to be uncomfortable, just don't avoid this season of preparation. If you do, you'll miss the best of what lies ahead. Fall into His plans for you. Rest and allow the Holy

Spirit to cultivate the seeds of spring God is planting inside you. God's best season for you is yet to come.

Lessons from Plan A

When life is about how you handle Plan B.

Throwing in the Towel: Token of defeat.

Sometimes, difficulties appear too great, and we just want to throw in the towel.

I am an adventure-seeking, dare-taking, living-life-on-the-edge person. There's no roller coaster, drop zone, skydiving experience that's even raised my heart rate one beat. I awake every morning insisting that whatever happens happens. I have no plans, but I long to breathe in the next outrageous challenge.

Every word in the paragraph above could not be further from the truth—except the words, "I awake every morning." I wish I was at least a little adventurous, but I'm not. I consider it brave when I move my beach chair in and out with the tide as the waves brush gently over my toes, eyes trained on the ocean for possible jellyfish attacks.

I find clarity in documenting my plans on my phone. It's much more rewarding to mark plans on the calendar that hangs on the refrigerator. It's there that I see my goals several times each day, checking off each day's events. That said, I often move goals, plans, and events to the next available day. Checking them off gives me a sense of accomplishment, but not so much when I move Plan A to another day, making it Plan B.

Depending on what interrupted my plans, I can become frustratedly off-balanced, especially if those plans are for good, productive activities. I don't mind interruptions to house-cleaning chores, but I hate interruptions that stop me from helping someone or reaching personal goals.

When I realize I won't accomplish a day's goals, I want to

give up. After all, they were good—even godly!—plans. Given a few minutes, I can put my day's expectations into perspective.

Are my daily plans so important that an interruption is a big deal? No. So why do interruptions turn into frustration and weariness?

Galatians instruct us to not grow weary in doing good. So, why do I feel like throwing in the towel? As I study His Word, I'm reminded of the story of the sower. Some are called to plant the seed, while others water or cultivate, and still others harvest. Each task can be tiring. If I'm planting seed after seed and don't see the fruit of my labor, I grow weary, thinking my efforts are meaningless. This is when God, the Master Gardener, reminds me of my purpose in His garden.

I'm accountable to plant the seed, while others do their part. It is God who gives the increase. It's His garden, and I'm blessed to be a small part of the process. His perfect plan far exceeds my goals. I'll go to Him when I feel weary. It's there that the towel is not thrown in but waved high in victory.

Prayer: *Is it you, God, who canceled my Plan A? Is it to send me in a different direction? Is it to avoid danger or perhaps heartbreak? Is it to catapult me into a better Plan A, your perfect Plan A? Are my motives pure or self-centered? Am I self-absorbed with the feeling of reward I sense when doing good?*

Father, is my weariness the result of thinking what matters to me is so important that an interruption is as aggravation? If so, then I repent and seek Your forgiveness. May I respond with the fruit of Your Spirit: love, gentleness, meekness, kindness, and patience.

I pray for my friends who are reading this lesson. If they experience the same, may they not give up. Propel us toward pure godly goals, planting seeds for Your harvest. Let us be known to You as faithful sowers who fight the good fight.

Don't throw in the towel, friend. Use it to wipe your brow. Tuck it in your pocket and get up. Move toward the center of the ring. God is in your corner. With Him by our side, we will not retreat. We will not give up. We will stay in the fight and wave our towel as a sign of Christ's victory!

Lessons from the Pond

Kindness: Loaning someone your strength instead of reminding them of their weakness.

Confession: Insert multiple eye rolls. I openly confess that I'm one of the drivers who grips the steering wheel a little tighter. My eyes roll and my heart rate increases as I wait for one or thirty geese to slowly.cross the road on their way to nowhere. Unrelated question: Why can't geese fly across the road?

These geese don't seem to care about all the people who are late for work, trying to get their children to school on time, or—like me—just want to get on with the day's plans. I don't want to see any of these little creatures harmed. I want them out of my way!

It was a beautiful sunny day, the first time we left the house for a couple of days. My husband, Larry, and I decided to get a sandwich and sit in the car by a pond. We wanted to sit quietly, taking in the calm and sunshine. As we approached, geese were everywhere: in the pond, on the grass, and covering the parking lot. As I maneuvered around them carefully, I wondered if I'd be able to escape by the same narrow route. Willing to take the risk, I pulled in view of the pond, and we began our in-car picnic.

Glancing toward our exit, I noticed a lonely goose approaching us, barely on the grass. He balanced awkwardly on the edge of the parking lot curbing. One look proved something was wrong with his wobbling approach. The poor goose had a broken leg. It was attached but totally snapped. Yet, he faithfully marched toward the other geese.

My eyes were no longer rolling. They were full of tears. I wondered what I could do. Was there a vet or animal control I could call to bring aid to this poor little goose? He would never make it down the steep hill to the pond for relief.

More questions flooded my thoughts.

Do geese show pain in their facial expressions? It didn't seem like it. Why didn't he cry out? He never made the slightest sound. Maybe he used all his strength to keep moving forward.

Did he belong to the group flying in their perfect V-shape pattern? Could he fly at all? Or was his family the group in the pond? How would he ever make it to them? Did he belong to the group wandering the parking lot? Were they looking for him?

Perhaps his family were nestled in the warm grass and sunlight.

As he inched closer to us, the poor thing showed pain for the first time. Cautiously, he leaned his head over the edge of the curb and sipped drops of dirty water from a tiny puddle in the asphalt. Each time he lifted his head to swallow, he seemed thankful to find relief from his journey. He dipped down two more times, until the tiny water supply was deplenished. He then maneuvered his broken leg under his body and sat down. Still no sound.

Suddenly, from the flock feasting in the grass, a goose turned his attention to the lonely, exhausted goose. Step by step, this second goose crept toward the wounded goose. It was the same maddeningly slow stroll used in front of speeding cars.

What would the second goose do upon reaching the wounded animal? I wasn't sure if more harm would occur or how the second goose could help. Then came the lesson from the pond.

The Responding Goose

The approaching goose seemingly couldn't help. It couldn't relieve the other goose's suffering. It couldn't fix the broken leg, bring clean water to relieve the dehydration, or call on a greater source for help. Yet, maybe that's the one thing that happened. The Word says God is aware of even the falling of a sparrow. So maybe that goose came knowing the Creator was aware and there to bring His presence where *brokenness* was unfixable.

As the goose came within two feet of the suffering goose, it turned its head, honked softly twice, then turned all attention to the wounded partner. Then it sat down facing the suffering goose. The soft honk attracted several other geese. None of them passed the calling goose. They all sat down, facing their wounded friend.

I'm forever thankful knowing I can *softly* call on friends to help; come sit with me to keep a prayerful vigil. These friends may not be present physically, but they come in prayer. Like the injured goose, sometimes all I need is to know you're there behind me, ready to support me in my difficult times. Like this goose, there is nothing else we can do but pray. There is also nothing we need more.

I ache for those who have not found their *flock*. My call rings out from our small group. At times, I am the wounded goose that knows, 'If only I can find my family, I'll find what I need: them."

More Lessons from the Pond: The Wounded Goose

God showed me additional lessons from the wounded goose. In no particular order, they include:

1. There are circumstances when physical, emotional, or spiritual pain is so deep that all your strength is consumed. Crying out isn't an option. We know we can't fix the problem, and neither can anyone else. In these moments, come sit alongside me. Bow down to the Creator. Wait with me.

2. The wounded often seek solitude, pushing away the very people who can carry them into God's Presence. Yet, the wounded goose understood his most desperate need was not the murky water in the parking lot drain, but his family. His need was to not be alone in his suffering. "For who can bandage and care for their own bleeding wounds? Isn't it true that a double cord (when two stand back to back to guard) can conquer, but a triple-braided cord is all the stronger?" (Ecclesiastes 4: 9–12)

3. The wounded goose sipped with thankfulness. I don't know if geese can show feelings with facial expression, but I witnessed thankfulness. As he raised his head, tilting his beak to the sky, I saw movement in his neck as the water trickled down. He sipped twice. After the first sip of stagnant water, he went back down for the last remaining drops. He was thankful, no matter the dirty taste or temperature on that hot, muggy day. Thankful.

4. The wounded goose kept marching. Putting his body weight on a snapped leg had to be incredibly painful. But he didn't stop. He didn't hesitate. He kept his steady

march forward. He kept his eyes on the goal and moved toward his beloved.

When someone is hurting, it's natural to want to rush in and fix it all by wiping away pain, suffering, and struggles from health issues. I know I want to do so. Yet, most of the time, I can't. That hurts most—I can't fix it. However, I can call out to friends. I can bring what small amount of comfort I have to offer.

I can give all my love, energy, and time to make things better. Yet, I'm limited. Very limited. I can't fix it.

Brokenness is perhaps the deadliest wound. Only God can heal. Only God can bring ashes to life.

God, I'm pressing forward. Moving on toward my Beloved.

I can't find words to express how deeply those moments touched my heart. It all occurred in less than 10 minutes, but the lessons have stuck. Since that day, I've thought about those geese often. How they know kindness: Loaning someone your strength instead of reminding them of their weakness.

God was preparing me through these geese.

About three weeks after this precious lesson, I watched my partner wounded, yet again. There was nothing I could do to help relieve the pain and heartache, as he wobbled toward relief. But I could be kind. I could sit beside him offering my strength until he regained his own.

It sounds admirable. It's not. It's exhausting. It's heart wrenching. It's frustrating. It causes sleepless nights and days. It's a paradox. It costs so much, yet it costs nothing. All I do is sit, watch, keep guard, and encourage, confident that the Creator knows and is present.

So, we continue to sit beside green pastures, feasting on the riches of His provisions. We rest beside still waters with thankful hearts, sipping in the waters of strength. It is His presence that brings the refreshing waters of peace. He restores our souls. We need nothing more.

Lessons from a Broken Heart

Disappointed: Sad or displeased that someone or something has failed to fulfill one's hopes of being realized.

After years of praying, yes about twenty years, the past nine months have brought it all to a heartbreaking halt. When others see my eyes fill with tears, they assume it's about cancer. I've allowed tears to fall about this illness only once. That was after realizing the dark moist dots on the floor were my burnt skin falling as it healed from a month of radiation treatments. I'll let others think cancer is the reason. I'll not respond otherwise. Cancer is rather simple compared to this kind of pain. It's personal and not my story to tell, so details will be kept in my bruised heart.

How could years of praying, based on the Word of God, go so wrong? I understand free will and man's right to choose. Yet, what do I do with all the shocking and disappointing pain? It was first on my lips in the morning and last at night, not to mention the hours during the day, crying out to God for change. The grief was so intense I didn't want to sleep, knowing I would dream about the facts of that day and awaken to the reality that it was all too true.

I didn't share it with my family or closest friends. *Don't tell and maybe it won't really happen.* Grief became something I felt, smelled, and tasted. Grief. What a limited word to describe a crushed heart.

Imagine my surprise when God spoke to my heart, asking me this question: "Are you disappointed in Me?"

Whoa! I wasn't expecting that, and I was unsure how to answer. My first thoughts were that I couldn't be disappointed in God. But I waited. Searched my heart. Answered with what

I thought was an honest, yet broken response. "No," I said. "Are you disappointed in me?" I thought I was being honest, but I later learned I wasn't being truthful even with myself.

I didn't stop there. I pleaded with Him for answers. "Did I do all that I was supposed to do?" I asked "Did I pray the right prayers? What more could I possibly have done to prevent this?"

His answer came back clearly as well. "Your responsibility is to pray and love well. I gave you *so, sew, sow love* as your word for 2023. Now you see what will be required of you. You are not the Holy Spirit. You cannot accomplish what only He can do. This may not end the way you prayed, but I'm doing a greater work that you cannot see or hear or understand right now. But in time—My timing, you will see My hand at work. I'm not disappointed in you either. Let go of this pain, the grief of disappointment."

God is stretching, pulling my faith and trust in Him to a higher level. Grateful as I am, it's like I'm being torn rather than just pulled. Exercise can bring healthy tears to muscle fibers. The healing can be extremely painful. Yet, the result is stronger muscles. Breaking and tearing our emotions can bring about the same healthy repair. Though it hurts, the healing creates a stronger godly character within me. This new strength is developed for a purpose greater than my ability to comprehend. So, press on. More tearing. More healing. More strength.

Are you disappointed? Disappointed in yourself, others, or perhaps even God? When crushing grief comes into our lives, we search for reasons why. Whose fault is this? Is it mine, the person causing the grief, or is it God? It's our nature to look for blame. One of my doctors gave me an article about how Christians handle cancer. They blame God for not keeping them safe from cancer or they blame themselves for somehow causing it. I fell into the latter group. Surely, I didn't handle grief well this time, so this is the result. It's not God's fault or the issue that brought on the grief. Even as I write this, the battle is fresh, and He's still revealing His plan for me.

This life is not an episode of *Let's Make a Deal*. We can't trade one challenge for another. I know that, yet that desire came to me. Realizing quickly that's not how it works didn't change the fact that I would try. I'd gladly take on my cancer battle if it would change the situation with the ones I love. But again, that's not how it works. What is exchangeable is the growth God asks of me and in me. I was given the opportunity to exchange grief for more trust. More faith in Him to do what only He can accomplish.

Come on up. Reach a little higher. His arms are already outstretched, reaching to me. Like a father with his child, knowing I'm weak and limited, He holds onto me.

What do I do with the deep cry and bruising of my heart when prayers seemingly go unanswered? I've come to accept that He may or may not answer my prayers the way I hoped. He is not my personal genie in a bottle. He is my Shepherd. The One who leads me through the valley of the shadow of death. He does not always keep me out of the shadow of death, He always holds me *through* it. I will not fear. He knows the pathway. I choose to follow closely and securely behind Him. I'll keep asking and trusting, not afraid to stay the course, not afraid to ask Him for more relief from my grief and fear.

I'm learning that God allows disappointment to catapult me to a higher level of trust in the Provider Shepherd.

How are you today, reader? Are you being crushed with disappointment? Do you have more questions than answers? Let's both stop and confess our weaknesses to Him, for He knows and cares. He's the Good, Kind Shepherd, who binds up the brokenhearted and brings peace to the weary soul. Let's climb onto the lap of our Heavenly Father, for that is where you and I will find rest and strength for the journey.

Lessons from Written in Love

Introduction to So, Sew, Sow Love

2022 ended with God leading me to focus on one word for 2023: *Love.* It felt so broad and challenging to define. It remains a goal of which I've barely scratched the surface. I began thinking about love in three terms: *so* love, *sew* love, and *sow* love.

This year provided me opportunity after opportunity in which it was a struggle to love. Loving people who love me came easily. Loving people I had helped on some level—counseling or with prayer—was also easy. After all, we connected out of their need, and they required compassion and time, both of which I was more than willing to offer. As I became more aware of their need for words of encouragement, I made a purposeful effort to ensure my words of affirmation reached not just their ears but their hearts. It blessed me more than anyone I contacted. They thanked me for my words, and even if they didn't, it didn't matter. I reached out to them because it was in my heart to do so. There was no need for a reciprocal response.

But loving someone only to have that love rejected, minimized, or abused was unexpected. It brought out a deeper need for God's love or work in and through me.

Obviously, God had me in training school. He loved me enough to be my Master Teacher. I understood that the upcoming lessons would be difficult.

That challenge rose to a new height I didn't anticipate. Suddenly, it was a struggle to love even myself with that same level of love. I can't explain how difficult it was in my marriage and family. Love for others wasn't at a high level of expectation, yet for myself and my family, it was on a level ten: inTENse. I chased that level of love but fell short time after time.

I discovered—perhaps due to the cancer I endured this year—that I needed love expressed in new ways. Words of affirmation became vital. I longed to hear others say, "I love you. Thank you for all you do that no one sees or acknowledges." I've never needed these words so badly. I didn't want them shouted from the mountaintop or written on social media, but I needed to hear them privately and spoken sincerely.

Hence, I began my first class:

Lesson from Written with Love: So Love

"For God so loved the world that He gave His only son."
(John 3:16)

So: To such a great extent.

Lesson one: Don't expect others to speak your love language. We give and receive love in different ways. During this time, I realized I speak two love languages: words of affirmation and quality time. Like most people, I want to receive love in the same manner that I give it. Perhaps as you read this devotional, you'll find your level of love needs a little boost, too. I found these few thoughts a good starting place.

- End a quarrel with a soft answer.
- Find the time to seek out a forgotten friend.
- Dismiss suspicion, replace it with trust, and try to understand the other.
- Forgo a grudge and forgive an enemy.
- Examine your demands on others. See beauty and wonder in them and discover their love language (it might be very different from yours).
- Be kind, be gentle, and develop an attitude of gratitude.
- Laugh a little. Laugh a little more.
- Speak love, speak it again, speak it once more.

Lesson from Written with Love: Sew Love

Sew: To join, fasten, or repair something by making stitches with a needle and thread; the activity of making single threads become a part of the whole.

My mom was an incredible seamstress. She worked for a company that made leisure suits for men. Those of you under fifty will need to look up that famous design wear. She did it without a pattern.

Growing up, I seldom received a store-bought dress. I never missed out, because what my mom made was always better and more beautiful. Unfortunately, that area of creativity was not passed down to me. Two of my sisters gained all Mom's talent and then some. I seldom attempt to even sew on a missing button due to high school trauma. I'd bring a garment home only to have Mom tell me to rip that out and redo it. The next day, I'd face my home-ec teacher, who echoed my mom: "You needed to rip that out and redo it." The cycle repeated itself until holes grew so large no amount of sewing could repair the material.

Romans 9:3 reveals that Paul *sew* loved his fellow Israelites. He was so compassionate and genuine that he offered to separate himself from Christ—if such a thing were possible—for the salvation of his fellow Jews. Pause and consider the results of such love. Can you imagine the depth of love required to tear away your place in heaven in order to weave another into your spot? We seldom allow someone to break in line in front of us at the grocery store, nevertheless give up heaven for them.

Paul knew it was not part of God's salvation plan that we

tear ourselves away from Him that another might take our place. It's impossible. Jesus is that sacrifice that opened Heaven. We can make no such sacrifice. But Paul loved others so much that he removed himself from life's benefits in order to win others to Christ. May you and I love others at such a depth that we, too, are willing to separate ourselves from what we want in order to weave others into God's family.

Can you see your heavenly garment as it is wrapped around you? It will be embellished with jewels of souls on that day of reward. Our exuberant joy will not be for the beauty of the robe but for the faces of those brought into the kingdom, saying, "Thank you for sewing me into the body of Christ."

> **Prayer:** *Dear Heavenly Father, may Your love be deeply threaded into my every thought, word, and deed. Help me to give up what is in my best interest for the salvation of others. Create in me a love so genuinely full of compassion that others only see You, causing them to desire to be woven into the Kingdom of Heaven.*
> *Don't allow a rotten thread of evil, deceit, jealousy, or slander to weave its way into my life. May my words and actions be filled with compassionate love for fellow believers and for the lost. Amen.*

Lesson from Written with Love: Sow Love

Sow: Plant seeds by scattering them over the earth.

How beautiful are the feet of those who bring the Good News! (Isaiah 52:7)

My paternal grandfather was a farmer. He rotated crops without the advice of agriculturists or the internet. He knew his land. He loved and took care of it. Life experiences and wisdom made him an excellent meteorologist. Grandpa gave sound advice about the next day's weather and how to dress for it. He was never wrong. He knew the exact time to plant and waited wisely for the perfect time to harvest.

My favorite memory on Grandpa's farm was harvesting potatoes. Loved that day!

With bare feet and a sack over our shoulders, my siblings and I walked behind the tractor picking up potatoes. It was better than any Easter egg hunt. The feel of the warm, brown soil was better than the best pedicure. Everything about it was a game. Who got the biggest potatoes, the smallest, a double header, or the weirdest shaped one? One might think I'd hate potatoes today, but it remains my favorite side dish in any shape or form.

Grandma was a hard worker, too. I remember being sick around her only once. I didn't dare get sick as she would brew some kind of root-based tea. If she went walking into the woods, we knew it was time for some kind of tonic. Any condition that couldn't be healed with one of her concoctions didn't need healing anyway.

She also had a wonderful talent for sewing. She made her own simple clothes, but what I remember most was her ability to repair shoes. Most of my shoes were similar to ballet slippers—soft, silky material with cardboard soles. If I got a hole in my shoes or the elastic band stretched out of shape, could I get new shoes? Oh, I think not. Mom would send me on the 750-step walk up the road to Grandma's house. (Yes, I counted every step.) I'd watch with gratefulness and amazement as Grandma traced the shape of my foot onto cardboard. Then she'd glue or sew the material to the bottom of my shoe. Sometimes she didn't use glue or thread. She just slipped the new material in and set it on top of the worn out sole. What talent!

My family planted thankfulness into my life. I never realized we were poor growing up. Even today, I don't remember childhood as a time of not having enough. We had more than enough. My dad had an ongoing joke about what kind of potatoes or beans Mom was preparing for dinner. He always added, "Tomorrow is the day we get to have both for supper." He made everything peaceful, reassuring, and funny. He was the corniest teller of dad jokes that has lived or ever will.

Dad and Mom planted peace and love into our hearts and minds.

There are seven siblings in my family. We are so alike, yet vastly different on many levels. We are as far from perfect as any family could be, but what we are harvesting are the crops taken from seeds planted generously in our lives. There wasn't yelling, fighting, or drama in our lives. We were raised with godly values but seldom in church. As a young child, I often wondered what knowing Jesus was really like. I was 17 years old and one of the last in my family to come to Jesus, but I'll be eternally grateful that my family prepared the soil of my heart to accept the seed of salvation planted patiently all those years before.

As I reflect on those cardboard shoes, I'm reminded of God's call on my life to sow love and walk with beautiful feet spreading the Gospel of Good News. Take a few moments to look at your feet. Are they beautiful? Are they sowing seeds of the Good News? Are you leaving behind footprints of faith, hope, and—the greatest of all—love?

Lessons from
Walk a Mile in My Shoes

Empathy: The ability to share another's emotional experiences which include affection, gratitude, sympathy, and compassion.

While reading these simple lessons, you might be tempted to skip this one. To be completely honest, I'd like to skip it, too. It's been on the back burner of my journal for weeks with a note to "Work on this someday."

Today is someday.

The title of this entry is better explained as "Empathy in Suffering." Call me a wimp, a weak Christian, whatever you wish, but I don't want to suffer. I've always wanted the life of June and Ward Cleaver. (Again, those of you under fifty will need to look into the TV archives of 1957 under the show titled *Leave It to Beaver*.)

June walked around in a perfectly pressed 1950's dress, wearing heels and pearls. She never broke a sweat as she vacuumed her immaculate house. Her biggest challenge was watching how her husband, Ward, would handle Beaver's latest nothing burger problem.

Have you ever looked at pictures on social media or glanced at your family and friends only to think, "They really have it so good. Their life has been so blessed, so easy. God has promoted them to an amazing level. Looks like everything is going their way."

The problem is we don't know the path they had to walk. I don't have the slightest clue what June Cleaver faced in her real life. I look at picture-perfect families and wonder what I'm doing wrong. I don't know the struggles of TV pastors who seem to have it all together and every word from their lips is golden. I don't know the price they had to pay and may still be paying for that level of anointing.

Until we've walked a mile in their shoes, we don't see the price of suffering that propelled someone to their current place. Therefore, use caution when you desire to walk in someone else's shoes. The path may be dimly lit and treacherous.

I'm sure my years of teaching cause me to look at the word *empathy* and see the word *path*: the direction in which a person is moving. All we view is a sliver of someone's current situation. Developing empathy creates a lifestyle of thankfulness and appreciation in all parts of our lives, for large and small things alike.

Before we prepare to walk in someone else's shoes, let's slip off our sandals for a good pedicure. I seldom treat myself to one because it feels so self-serving to expect someone to wash and care for my feet.

The first time someone got on their knees and washed my feet wasn't in a salon. I attended a ladies meeting where it was announced there would be a foot washing. I tried not to look shocked, but I wondered how to escape this awkward situation. I'd heard of a foot-washing service but never participated in one. Jesus washed the feet of His disciples, but I wanted no part of it that night.

I looked for the least disruptive way to walk out. It wasn't going to be easy. I sat in a circle of chairs with no outlet. I felt all eyes were on me. Would these ladies let me escape? Then I remembered I was the guest speaker. There was no option. I had to participate.

I hoped a total stranger would wash my feet. I didn't want someone I knew to humble herself by slipping my shoe off, praying over me, placing my foot in the small plastic tub, and drying off my foot. But the lady who invited me, the pastor's wife, grabbed my foot. I tried praying for her as she washed my feet, but she looked up at me. "No," she whispered, "allow me this honor. This is for you."

I share this to introduce you to another humble, soul-foot washing I received this week. Over the past several days, a female acquaintance began texting me. "Why is it every morning when I begin to pray I see your face and the need to pray for you?" she asked. "May I call you to pray?" I told her to call. I was facing several major issues and needed prayer. Yet, I was uncomfortable. Over the past years, she's experienced horrific suffering that continues to this day. I should be sprawled out on her doorstep praying and doing everything I could think of to help her. Yet, she was going to pray for me.

Here's one of the greatest daughters in His Kingdom, calling me to slip off my shoe and preparing to drench me in love and prayer. How could she pray about my suffering when hers is so severe?

She called. She prayed. She bathed my soul and heart.

I now share this small part of the encouragement she placed before me. Although I only listed them, each could be an entire book.

We must realize there is purpose in our suffering.

1. Suffering reminds us of Christ's suffering for us.
2. Suffering keeps us from pride.
3. Suffering causes us to look beyond this brief life.
4. Suffering gives us opportunity to prove our faith to others.
5. Suffering gives God the opportunity to demonstrate His power.

This life is not all there is. There is life after death. Knowing we will live with God forever in a place without sin and suffering can help us live above the pain we face in this life.

Until you walk in the shadow of another's suffering path, emPATHy hasn't developed. Empathy leads you down the pathway of compassion and an attitude of gratitude. Together they propel you toward action. My dear friend said it best: "Gratitude takes your mind off personal suffering, replacing your thoughts, thus, your actions. The service itself becomes healing for the one doing it. A holy conundrum, if you will."

Leaving the grip of grief—not the grief itself but its crippling hold—is a miracle.

You'll find after performing an act of service that you are the one being healed. Your bruised heart will sense the healing oil of the Holy Spirit being dropped tenderly into your innermost being. Action by action, drop by drop, empathy in suffering has its full circle. It's by divine design.

I wish you could sit with my friend and hear her story, if you could take it in. Most can't. You would leave with more empathy than you can scarcely contain. It wouldn't sprout from hearing the horror of her grief, but rather the power of her words and prayers. That power would change your life forever. I dare not touch her story with meaningless words. However, this I know for sure:

You wouldn't be satisfied with walking in empathy. You would run with all your might!

There is a test in a testimony with a price many are not willing to pay. Yet, the Bible tells us that suffering is not just a part of life. It's a place of honor.

Suffering produces scars. Scars begin the healing process when compassion and gratitude are generously poured out. Healing creates more empathy. Empathy is the fullness of Christ in action. (If you like to highlight statements that require more time to process, highlight away!)

I end this lesson with one more thought. My long-suffering, prayer-warrior friend shared that there are seven words nobody wants to hear at a funeral. Those words:

"Let me know what I can do."

These words require the one suffering to take action, to call and tell you what to do. Empathy says, "Go buy paper plates, napkins, and cups, along with plastic forks and knives. Then change those seven words to these:

"Chicken dinner is on your front porch."

Perhaps add seven more:

"And I'll be back soon with more."

Do you see how empathy calls for action? *Empathy* requires you to create the *path.*

I can't begin to put myself in my friend's place, yet empathy takes hold, and I do what needs to be done. I take off my June Ward dress and wrap the towel of a servant around my waist, exchange those high heels for bare feet that spread the Good News, and replace "Let me know" with "I know, because I know God's heart."

What path of empathy will you walk today?

"Guide me into the paths that please You, for I take delight in all that You say." (Psalm 119: 35)

Lessons from When the Doorbell Rang

Rudder: The primary control used to steer ships, submarines, and aircrafts through a fluid medium, usually air or water. A rudder is usually 1/10,000th of the size of the vehicle it is directing. It doesn't move the ship but rather directs its course.

My dad wore steel-toe shoes at work. It was required for his protection. Heavy equipment could easily cause great damage if dropped on his feet. I wish I had those steel boots on now, because this lesson drops heavily onto my big toe!

Those who have met my husband know that he is a kind man full of wisdom and generosity. Many think he walks on water, and on most days I agree. However, I've also seen him walk on my last nerve! I've done more than my share of stepping on his though.

One day, the words of my mouth and meditations of my heart were displeasing to God and about to bubble out. Okay, they weren't going to bubble out. They were going to gush like a geyser. These thoughts had been building all day and were giving signs of a major eruption. Once erupted, this hot spring wasn't going to be a pretty sight.

I've never used bad language, but I rehearsed my points. If Larry pushed the issue one more time, I was prepared to share. I stepped outside to catch my breath and regain control of what I was about to say. Standing in the warmth of the afternoon sun, I suspected, would help me realize the issue didn't really matter. I was wrong.

Once I stepped outside, I began repeating—out loud—why

I was right. It sounded good and right to me. Just then, the doorbell rang.

Our youngest son gifted us a ring bell system. It has been nice seeing who is at the door before I open it. It has its disadvantages also, as my Apple Watch notifies me every time someone in our city loses or finds a dog or cat. For some reason, my neighbors lose their pets several times per day.

When my watch notified me that someone was at my door, I ignored it. I knew I had set it off. So I stayed put, as the camera recorded me standing there. Thankfully, I had the sound turned off! God used that moment to show me how awful it would be to record the words of my mouth and the thoughts of my heart. Unlike deleting notifications, words can't be gathered easily. It would be like chasing falling leaves on a windy day.

Embarrassed, I asked God for forgiveness and strength to control the rudder of my tongue. That rudder has no power to move the ship, but it controls the direction the ship travels. The entire crew depends on the rudder to do its job. Should the rudder break, expect a violent change in the planned direction, sending everyone into turmoil.

Prayer: *My Dear Heavenly Father,*
Thank you for loving this daughter so much that You discipline me with such care. I cherish Your Word more than the finest gold. It is never bitter but brings my soul sweet redemption. My hidden flaws are recorded and Your kindness plays them back to me, giving me grace and mercy to repent. Give me more and more of Your strength to control this rudder, my tongue. Your Word tells me that I can have the mind of Christ. When I control my thought pattern, peace prevails. May I never damage my crew—those in my family and those You've given me to help guide. Your great

kindness projects them in a vision before me. May I never cause even one to go off course. May every movement of this ship be under Your devine direction and power.
Your Loving Daughter,
Sara Jane

Lessons from the Butterfly Effect

Metamorphosis: The process of transition from an immature form to an adult in two or more distinct stages. It involves a change of the nature of a thing or person in a completely different form by natural or supernatural means.

In times of chaos, the butterfly effect is when a small change in one state determines a larger result difference in a later state. If I skip what it takes to make a small change now, I negate the results of a future supernatural gain.

There are few things I'd dread more than participating in an Escape Room adventure. Granted, I'm the CEO of boring competitions. However, placing me in a locked room with a limited amount of time to get out—well, just go ahead and lock me inside a coffin. It all means the same to me.

Life can be that way—locked into a situation, an issue, a wrapped tight dark place. I want to escape those, too. Often the struggle doesn't last long. A solution, a way of escape comes my way. But, oh!—the times when there is no way to break free. I can't find the code to unlock the barricaded door to peace. I want out! And I want out now!

This cocoon stage is dark. I can barely breathe. I'm pressed in on every side. Depression and panic become the enemy inside my space. Although there seems to be no room for movement, I feel them brush against me as I strive to keep them away. My skin crawls from the hot breath as they pass around me.

If I can't get out by myself, perhaps someone can break down the door and set me free. But what if this assistance causes me harm? What if the process of metamorphosis is the plan for me? Can escaping the darkness of the chrysalis hinder the beauty of the future stage God has planned for me? Is this part of the butterfly effect? Is the battle part of the plan for flying free, wings outstretched and fluttering among the glorious morning dew? Can there be joy and beauty without the fight to be free?

Many people are fascinated by the soundless flight of butterflies. One of my granddaughters can stretch out her arm, and butterflies land on her as if they've found the fairest of fragrant blossoms. Some view butterflies as a reminder of a loved one who has passed away, a sign that those loved ones are watching over them. Butterflies represent comfort, hope, and positivity. I'm drawn to butterflies' unique features and stages of life. They taste food with their feet.

Their eyes consist of over 6,000 lenses, and they can see ultraviolet light. While in the egg stage, they are the size of a pinhead. The caterpillar is the stage of eating. What a yummy stage! Yet it is the cocoon/chrysalis stage that is the most daunting. This stage takes place hidden under a leaf or in the underbrush. It seems nothing is happening. Yet, it is the place of endurance and growth. In this stage, the butterfly twists to escape. This twisting releases a chemical that strengthens the wings. The movement pumps fluid into the wings, causes the wing to expand, and develops necessary muscles to live the life for which the creature was created.

What if someone, although well meaning, tries to help the escape process? The assisted escape is the butterfly's doom. The wings will fight to unfold, but they will not expand. That weakened butterfly will be helpless, subject to the harsh environment and predators.

So, leave me in the cocoon as long as necessary. Let me develop according to Your perfect plan, O God, my Creator. Let me develop strong physical, spiritual, and emotional muscles in order to fly into the glorious paths You've prepared for me. The latter stage of the butterfly effect produces life, peace, joy, and—most of all—the freedom to fly among others and point them to You.

God was there inside the chrysalis all the time. I was never alone. He was waiting for me to remember that I had been given the catalyst needed to set me free.

As I twisted inside, praise came from a secret place inside me. Praise became the same release as the chemical produced by the butterfly. Oh, it was a process. But as praise and worship became authentic praise and true worship, the chrysalis began to crack. More praise, more worship, more cracks formed. My wings lifted in praise and became stronger and stronger.

Like the magnificent wings of a butterfly, praise appeared as waves of spectacular colors ascending to the skies. They expanded higher and higher until I took flight into His arms of mercy and grace. The fragrance of praise rose to the heavenly throne and carried me there, the place I longed to be: in His presence.

The butterfly effect reminds us that it's never too late to transform our lives.

> *"Now, if anyone is enfolded (cocooned, my translation) into Christ, he has become an entirely new person. All that is related to the old order (former life stage) has vanished. Behold, everything is fresh and new. And God has made all things new and reconciled us to Himself, and given us the ministry of reconciling others to God." (2 Corinthians 5:17, The Passion Translation)*

> *"For you have acquired a new creation life, which is continually being renewed into the likeness of the One who created you; giving you the full revelation of God." (Colossians 3:10)*

Lessons from the Elephant in the Room

Memory: The faculty by which the mind stores and retains information.

Elephants never forget. They don't have the greatest eyesight in the animal kingdom, but they never forget a face. Research shows they are the only animal that can recognize their own faces in a mirror. I can't help but question how scientists can prove that, but the thought makes me smile. Sometimes I don't recognize myself in a reflection. Nevertheless, the elephant's memory is unforgettable. Yes, it's a corny, intentional play on words. I couldn't help myself.

An interesting event occurred inside the elephant sanctuary in Hohenwald, Tennessee. At the time, one of the female elephants had been in the sanctuary for twenty-three years. Sanctuary administrators were about to introduce another female elephant that, according to tracking records, caused sanctuary experts to believe the two had met at some point more than twenty-three years earlier. The researchers took precautions, unsure if the reunion would be one of hostility or joy. As anticipated, the reunion was unforgettable.

The two giant mammals bellowed and moved around with excitement. Using their trunks, they searched out the other's scars. With each recognition, the rejoicing of reunited friends grew. Their past remained secured in their memories.

I can't help but be curious. Did they once belong to the same herd? Had they defended one another? Had some of the battle scars been caused by members of their own herd or even each other? Were they part of the matriarch that stood shoulder to shoulder, encircling their sisters while protecting the birth of a calf or fighting off predators? Did they recognize the scars as marks of unflinching loyalty? Did the joy of seeing one another again outweigh the memory of former hurts? What incredible memories are forever stored within their sisterhood!

As the Holy Spirit dealt with me about recent emotional scarring, I searched my own memory bank. I've heard it said, "I'll forgive but I won't forget." I've never agreed with that statement, as I believe forgiving is a decision, while memory is more about emotions. Sometimes, forgiveness is a one-time commitment, but often it requires repeated resolve until a sin is truly forgiven and forgotten, with no emotional attachment.

For me, I know forgiveness has been completely achieved when I no longer give the past hurt the slightest thought. But therein lies my struggle. I have the habit of "nurse and rehearse." In my flesh, I long to give those who wrong me a piece (peace) of my mind! Fortunately, 2 Corinthians 10:5 interrupted the recording session. "Capture, like prisoners of war, every thought, and insist that it bow in obedience to the Anointed One." It took obedience and discipline on my part, but as soon as the rehearsal of what I'd like to say began recording, the Scripture raised its voice until my ungodly memory bank was placed behind locked doors, never to be unlocked into my thoughts again.

I'm honest with myself. There is a scar, a deep ugly scar. Here is what I've learned about scars. They can speak. They can tell the story of what occurred. If we open ourselves to others, others can witness our battle and see the scars. We can then encircle one another, rejoicing with the Victor who overcame.

There is another lesson I've learned about scars. They may remain, but they cause no more pain. When Jesus showed Thomas His crucifixion wounds, Jesus said, "Put your *finger* here in the wounds of my hand. Put your *hand* into my wounded side and see for yourself. Thomas, don't give in to your doubts any longer, just believe!" (John 20:27)

Some scars represent painfully small wounds: Put your finger here . . .

While others are so deep a hand can be placed entirely inside.

Both can be completely healed, allowing others to be restored by understanding you made it and they can, too.

Having a scar does not indicate the absence of forgiveness. It indicates the absence of pain. Forgiving is not only setting yourself free but also the person who wounded you. I've heard it said that forgiveness has little to do with the other person.

Jesus illustrated a deeper level of forgiveness and restoration. He made a way to show forgiveness to Thomas and open the door for Thomas to forgive himself. There are sweet memories that replace the thoughts of scarring. I won't let the scarring continue to embed itself into my storehouse of thoughts.

I set us both free.

Friend, are you hurting from a wound, a scar? Bring it to Jesus, who understands the hurt and disappointment. At the foot of the cross, your healing has been paid in full. Trust the Great Physician.

Lessons from the Shore

Exquisite: Marked by flawless beauty by the skills of the master's craftsmanship.

We all love miraculous testimonies. The challenge comes when nobody wants the "test" for the "imonies." I understand that's not a word, but it's true.

You don't get to your seventies without passing through the school of testing. I don't think I can categorize which test was the hardest. Several were major exams. The most recent one ranks somewhere near the top.

I never answer my phone if I don't recognize the number. Just a few days ago, that changed. This time, the Lord prompted me to answer, hearing in my spirit this comforting word: "Answer the call. This is what I've prepared you to hear. It's okay. I'm preparing inside you what you need for the journey."

The voice asked for Sara. I always know it's business if someone calls me by my first name. Only my dad got that privilege. Cautiously, the lady on the other end of the call tells me I need to come back for further testing. It sounded so simple, like she asked me to stop by for a glass of tea. "I'll be there," I replied.

Walking in, all the paperwork was different. "Oh, I see," I said to God. "This is what You prepared me to undertake." The Holy Spirit whispered into my heart two peaceful words: "It's okay." I echoed His responses: "Okay."

I confess, I longed to hear more, but I understood the "okay" didn't mean everything was all right. It meant He was with me, so I'd be okay. Submitting to the calm, I continued to fill out the paperwork.

As I write this, I'm only three weeks into my walk with breast cancer. Surgery takes place in a few days. There are moments when it hits hard. What is the mass inside my body? How did it enter? Why do I have so much pain? I love the beach, so the journey caused me to recall one of my favorite facts.

An exquisite pearl is produced within the body of an oyster after it is wounded. Sand or some object or toxin must enter its tender internal parts. Pearls are produced when pain is healed.

What if the greatest pain produces the most exquisite pearl? God never allows pain without purpose. A pearl is a healed wound.

"I am convinced that any suffering we endure is less than nothing compared to the magnitude of glory that is about to be unveiled within us. The entire universe is standing on tiptoe yearning to see the unveiling of God's glorious sons and daughters." (Romans 8:18–19)

Can you imagine that during your greatest sufferings, the *universe* is standing on tiptoes to see God's glory unveiled in you? Like the lifting of the bridal veil to see His glory produced on your face!

What wound is the Holy Spirit wrapping within you in order to produce His exquisite masterpiece? It will be a pearl of great price, a pearl that allows others to view His glorious power. Pause and give deep thought to the pearl being created inside your pain. I can almost see God's angels, whom He has given charge over you, standing guard ready to report on the exquisite pearl of healing within you.

Trust His Timing

"The steps of the God-pursuing ones follow firmly in the footsteps of the Lord, and God delights in every step they take to follow Him." (Psalm 37:23)

I had plans to leave town on March 31 for a week or two—not a vacation, but to help someone with their "internal wound." But I was stopped from going. Not by circumstances, but by the Holy Spirit.

My surgery date was set for March 31, the very day I planned to leave. Since I know our steps are directed by God, how could I possibly see that as a conflict but a *setup* by Him. God spoke to me that His Spirit can and will accomplish more than I could ever do. He's doing the wraparound love of wound healing no one else can do. Although my body shakes with concerns, I choose to trust Him.

Lessons from the First Grade Calendar

The month of March: In like a lamb, out like a lion.

The Lion and the Lamb: "He endured death as a lamb; He devoured it as a lion."—Augustine

As a former first grade teacher, I loved the month of March. It was filled with wonderful, fun activities: seasonal change, new plant and animal life, weather, predictions, math graphs, and St. Patrick's Day to name a few. Perhaps one of my favorites was graphing the weather predictions for the month of March. The students would predict on a weather graph if March would come in like a lamb and leave like a lion or visa versa. At the end of the month, we would review our predictions.

This year, I thought March came in like a lion and hopefully would leave like a lamb. My prediction proved incorrect. Larry was out of state on March 1, as I sat in the radiologist's office for my biopsy results. The report was that the mass in the left breast was cancer. Surgery was scheduled for March 31, thus deeming my "in like a lion out like a lamb" prediction incorrect. Surgery had to be the lion!

March proved a month of doctor after doctor, test after test. If the biopsy was cancerous, why not just do surgery and take it out? I had a lot to learn.

There was a lot of predicting to do. After each test, I waited for the results. Some came immediately, other results came days later, and some tests had to be repeated. The crazy part was that after the results came in, I had to predict which choice would be best for me concerning a surgery I had yet to undergo. Should I undergo lumpectomy or mastectomy? Have one breast or both removed? Which do I predict will be best for me later? Which surgeon? What hospital? What aftercare? What?!?

One thing I didn't predict was that I would be awake during the prep and planning procedures. Who thought of this stuff? Perhaps surgery is the lamb after all, and this part is the lion.

The only prediction I knew to be true was that I can't predict anything—not the next few seconds, and especially not the years to come. My decisions are based on the information at hand and the full assurance that my steps are ordered by God.

"The steps of the God-pursuing ones follow firmly in the footsteps of the Lord, and God delights in every step they take to follow him. If they stumble badly they will still survive, for the Lord lifts them up with his hands." (Psalm 37:23–24)

Psalm 29 opens with a majestic thunderstorm, the lion, and ends with peace, the lamb.

This Psalm records seven times how powerful the voice of God is as it echoes across the skies and seas. I can almost see each bolt of lightning as its jagged edges splinter the clouds. It is powerful, so bright and brilliant. I cover my ears to block out some of the force of the rumbling of thunder as it rolls into the distance until it can no longer be heard. The storm is to be revered and honored, not feared.

All creation responds, "Glory, glory, the God of glory."

The Psalm ends with peace. "Above the furious flood the Enthroned One reigns, the King-God rules with eternity at His side. This is the one who gives His strength and might to His people. This is the Lord giving us His kiss of peace."

It doesn't matter if our day begins or ends like a lion. God is

in control. He is the Lion and the Lamb.
He has promised us the kiss of peace.
My prayers are with you today as you face your storm.

Lessons from the Cancer Center Doorway

Courageous: Possessing or displaying courage; able to face and deal with fear or danger without flinching.

I stood frozen on the sidewalk, staring at the building's automatic doors opening to welcome me to the cancer center. Welcome? How can I walk through a doorway that opens so effortlessly?

Am I dreaming? Am I making this all up? Have I misunderstood?

Gently, God placed His hand on my back and whispered, "I'm going before you, behind you, and beside you. I am your Shield and the Lifter of your head. I have a plan bigger and greater than you. Walk in. The doors will automatically open before you. You only need to take a step."

My strength renewed as I stepped forward, ready to obey His voice. It is totally God when strength enters my heart while my feet shake beneath me. Courage is not the absence of fear but the presence of faith, knowing God will supply what is needed to face and move toward my giant. That courage seemed absent for only a moment. I'm sure I flinched. Yet, He graciously filled my reservoir.

When I walked into the room, I couldn't breathe. The air was heavy and warm, despite a cold rush from the air conditioner sending chills down my bare arms.

I felt so out of place, embarrassed that I'd overdressed for the occasion. Everyone else wore grays and browns, jeans and t-shirts. I waltzed in wearing spring colors—slacks and a blouse. I wondered why the colors I wore mattered. *Stop overthinking.*

Four other patients were in the waiting room. I may have flashed a smile. I'm not sure. Their glances moved from their folded hands long enough to catch a quick glimpse of me. Then their eyes shifted back to their laps. Without speaking, they said in unison, "Hi. Sorry you're here. Join us in the wait."

I felt guilty for looking so healthy. My heart was breaking.

Most others had bare heads wrapped in scarves and needed assistance when called by the nurse. I stood to open the door for a lady being brought out in a wheelchair. She was so thin that all I saw was the black material she was draped in from head to toe. If her shoes didn't poke out from her clothes on the footrest, I wouldn't have known she was there. I would have thought it was a blanket laying across the wheelchair frame. I made out her paper-thin skin, slender fingers, and fragile arm holding up her bowed head.

How dare I feel afraid. Look at these ladies.

I walked into the restroom to pull myself together.

There, God reminded me of His Word: "So do not fear for I am with you; do not be dismayed for I am your God. I will strengthen you and help you; I will uphold you with My righteous hand." (Isaiah 41:10)

How brave these precious women were to come for treatment day after day. Yet, I wasn't even on day one. "I'm here to meet the radiologist," I reminded myself. "No testing. No needles. No pain. Just here to listen. Take everything one step at a time."

I was four weeks out from breast cancer surgery, and this is the next step. We sat with the radiologist for about thirty minutes. Listening became more difficult than needle pricks.

At least with a needle, the pain ends in seconds. This pain would occur five days a week for five weeks—everyday, and with what effects?

I listened. Took notes. Yet, was I completely comprehending? I understood what was said, but who were we talking about?

I told myself, "You can do this."

I never ask, "Why me?" I only seek to follow the Shepherd so closely that I don't step off the edge into the plummeting valley below.

I looked around at the well-loved ladies. They are His children, the sheep of His pasture. They can do it. So can I.

I understood I was there because of the breast cancer diagnosis, but there was another reason. I was on assignment. I felt strongly that I ought not use my voice to share my love for Jesus. I was on assignment to love the staff. I didn't see the plan yet, but I knew He had one in mind. God always has purpose in the plan, so I resolved to walk this out. I wouldn't think only about myself. I would use the radiation time to pray for others. I wouldn't seek to get out of this.

I was determined from that day forward to enter the cancer center with joy.

While in prison, Paul wrote to encourage the church of Philippi about his heavenly joy while under the control of others. He didn't think only of himself or how to get out of jail. Paul recognized he was put there by God on purpose. What was meant to stop him actually served to advance the spread of the Good News. He understood, and it turned out for his deliverance and spiritual well-being.

Lessons from My Kitchen Table

Provision: The supplying of food, drink, or equipment, especially for a journey.

While trying to focus on morning devotions, I give in to the distraction of birds singing from my kitchen window. How busily they gather bits and pieces to build their nest! It's too soon for flowers to bud and birds to gather for their nest. It's chilly outside, with a high in the low forties.

Regardless of the stress of the seasonal changes, their song remains the same: joy-filled and grateful. They put into practice what I know: Things will change. This is only a season. What must not change is my song.

My song of praise.

My song of joy.

My song of loving God.

The song of love He sings back to me.

This is only a season. It's my season of waiting. Part of the provision of the Lord is the grace to wait. In the waiting, strength for the journey gets packed into our character. It takes time to develop.

I'm waiting through the long process of healing from cancer and the effects of radiation. Yet, that is not the valley of shadows that hurts most. My heart is broken and wounded from the deception and manipulation of a long-time friend. We're no longer friends, yet I will not view her as an enemy. She chose to be released from our relationship, so I'm learning to let her go. I pray I'll let go of it all. How else will I be able to please God and help those wounded more deeply than I? Like the burns from radiation, what can I really do?

Sometimes I can't distinguish the effects on my body and

mind from the results of radiation or wounds of the heart. In order to really heal, I bring myself to the prayer altar. As long as I try to fix the problem, I remain powerless. I can't. I won't. God is the provider of all things. Why worry about this life? He is all I need. He is my portion and provision.

Sing on my soul!

"This is why I tell you to never be worried about your life, for all that you need will be provided, such as food, water, clothing—everything your body needs. Look at all the birds—do you think they worry about their existence? They don't plant or reap or store up food, yet your heavenly Father provides them each with food." (Matthew 6: 25–27)

Are you wounded today? Does a broken relationship bring great sadness to your heart? As we pray over them together, healing will come. Perhaps like me, you find you can't change others' decisions, but you can change yours. Choose to love, pray, and keep the door of your heart open for healing. I'll join you.

Lessons from the Control Tower

It was never about the fork.

Control: The ability to influence or direct behavior or the course of events.

I became anxious as evening approaches. Why? Doesn't sunset happen every day at about the same time? I looked for distractions. I walked around, reached for my phone, checked the weather app. Sometimes, I even started organizing the pantry. What on earth? I face two hard events: cancer and personal loss, cancer being the least harmful.

My favorite times of day have always been early-morning sunrises and soft, comforting sunsets. Watching hues of pink and orange paint the skyline previously filled my cup. Why has this changed? In a few hours, my exhausted mind and body would succumb to sleep. But I didn't want to sleep. I didn't want another day to end, as it speeds the approach of more testing and treatments. I didn't want to be another day closer to feeling my heart crushed over events that bring on a family member's heartbreak. I couldn't control either of the events. I couldn't change it. I tried. It was like trying to stop the day's sunset from happening. I'm not able. Not even close.

I didn't want to sleep. When I did sleep, my dreams remained the same. I was going somewhere I didn't want to go. I knew it wouldn't end well, but I was the passenger. Someone else was driving. Someone else was in control. That someone took me against my will.

Today was filled with cancer doctors and blood tests. Another day of processing words I've never heard. Do I have a say or is this the way it is? Words tumbled across my mind like squares dropped from a Scrabble board. I was overwhelmed with others asking what was said when I couldn't process what I was told.

My husband and I ended the day by loading the dishwasher after dinner. I leaned over to place a fork in the dishwasher. He immediately pulled it out and put it into "the correct spot in the tray." I couldn't even control where a dirty fork goes! I left the room, crushed.

I climbed into bed and curled up into a ball. I covered my head and cried, prayed, slept, cried, prayed, and slept for three hours. God held me. Let me cry, pray, and sleep. Then, as the gentle Father that He is, His Spirit spoke to me.

"It's never about the fork, Jane," He said. "It's that you feel you have no control over anything happening."

The *fork* is in the place of cleansing. It doesn't matter if it's in the correct basket in the dishwasher. It will be cleaned and used again to serve its intended purpose: to bring nourishment to the body. I'm not in control. I'm only the instrument, the fork. God has placed me in the container He has planned for me. I'm here to serve my Master, and His purpose is to bring nourishment to the body of Christ. Cleanse me. Use me. Place me where You need me to serve. You are my Shepherd. I am not alone. Your mercy is falling, and your love is pouring out over me. It's cleansing every impurity from my body, mind, and soul. When I think I'm slipping, I know You are holding me close. If I fall, I will only fall into Your arms of love and safety.

I'm praying for you today, my friend.

"I cried out, 'I'm slipping!' but Your unfailing love, O Lord, supported me. When doubts filled my mind, Your comfort gave me renewed hope and cheered my soul." (Psalm 94:18–19)

Lessons from an "F" on my Report Card

Treasure: To keep carefully a very valuable object or item; precious metals, gems.

I was listening and worshiping the Lord when the Lord asked, "Are you being honest with yourself when you say you're not disappointed in Me?" My quiet internal answer rang out, "Yes, I am disappointed. I did my part. I prayed. I worked. I stayed the course. I believed. I trusted. Yet, it failed. It didn't work."

I still wouldn't admit I was disappointed that God didn't do what I prayed He would. Then this thought shot into my mind: "How, after all I've prayed (oh boy!), did He not do what I asked from day one? I prayed, 'Don't let us win others and lose our own family members.' They are my *treasures*. Yet, it seems the prayer wasn't heard or answered."

I confessed to myself and to God what He already knew, as He patiently waited for me to be honest with myself. Then and only then could I come before Him and be healed.

I was so deeply wounded by circumstances I didn't understand and why He didn't intervene. After all, this brokenness could not be His plan. I had scriptures, prayers, and words of promises for my children and their children. Why didn't it work? So yes, I'm disappointed. I failed. It failed to work. Now what else won't work out?

My trust and hope was eroding, being put to the test. My motives and sense of deserving something (for nothing) was laid out before me. All my righteous filthy rags were paraded before me with a smell beyond unpleasant. Failure, disappointment, and self-deserving have a distinctive odor. They stink!

I received a big, ugly F on my report card—filthy, failure, faithless, fragile.

The first time I gave a child an F on a report card, I worried. Would he understand it was the subject matter he didn't comprehend and that it did not label him a failure? This F on my report card was the opposite. It was about me personally. I was a failure. I failed the test of "where your treasure is, there is your heart."

"For your heart will always pursue what you value as your treasure." (Matthew 6:21)

There is an old song that says, "Turn your eyes upon Jesus. Look full in His wonderful face. And the things of Earth will grow strangely dim in the light of His glory and grace."

To see myself as God sees me is to look into His face, to gaze at my true treasure.

God's report is found in His Word. He calls me friend, faithful, fearless, forgiving, forbearing. He encourages me to look into His mirror, His Word, to see myself from His point of view, from the cross. He paid the price. Not me. He's the perfect treasured Lamb.

From Psalm 27:14, here's what I'm learning through it all.
- Don't give up.
- Don't be impatient.
- Be entwined as one with the Lord.
- Be brave and courageous.
- Never lose hope.
- Keep waiting. He will never disappoint.
- I'm back to being honest about disappointment.
- No. I'm not disappointed in God, and—praise God!— He's not disappointed in me.

Finally, I can heal. I'm not disappointed in myself. I don't have answers to my prayers, yet now more than ever my confidence is in Him. I trust him fully and completely to accomplish His plan, not mine. The F on my report card is revealed as fully trusting in my TREASURE.

Lessons from the Art Room

Modern art postcard.

Master Artist: Someone who knows exactly where to place brush strokes, whose apprentices are often called disciples.

I received a postcard today from my friend Madeline. She wrote:

Hello, Ms. Jane,
While going about my hectic Monday morning, I was look-
ing through my office supplies, and I ran across this old
beautiful museum card. Someone whispered, "Send it to
Jane."
I must have picked it up years ago at a museum in Florida.
My daughter loves art and so do I, but don't always know
what I'm looking at. I sat here and looked intentionally
and honestly I can not tell what is top or bottom of the
painting in this card. I just know it's beautiful. Sometimes
life is beautiful but it doesn't make sense, but Christians
can have the assurance and peace to know the Artist knew.
The Creator of our life knows how our beautiful life was
orchestrated. (Hebrews 12:2)

Today, they changed my body's position on the radiation table. My head was lower and my feet were raised higher. The change made me slightly dizzy.

I never open my eyes during radiation. I don't want to see the red beam cross my body, brushing me with its red paint. Even with my eyes closed, it's so bright I can tell when it moves to the right and when three red beams target me, hover over top of me, repeat the red flashes, then go to my left for three more beams. It only takes a few minutes, but it's becoming intense. Radiation moves subatomic particles of high-energy heat via light rays, and I'm the target.

Like the postcard from my friend, I get turned and painted with flashes of light. I'm not sure if I'm up or down. What picture will be my final outcome? What will this look like at the end of the month of painting?

I am on the eighth session, and blisters have formed and moved across my burnt armpit and breast. The exhaustion is challenging as well. I feel as if I've been in a swimming pool for hours. Stepping out, I feel the weight of water pulling me under.

The Destination worship team wrote an amazing song titled "Over Us."

Your mercy is falling.
Your love is pouring out over us.
Your Spirit is calling.
Your voice is singing life over us.

I play it every day before entering the cancer center: The worship team will never fully realize how much encouragement that song gave me. More than encouragement, actually. Walking into the cancer center, I ask God to place upon my heart the person who needs mercy and life to sing over them. I intentionally call out that person's name and needs while radiation pours over me.

I'm learning not to be concerned about the painting red beam. Rather, I'm learning to see it as God's mercy and love, as His voice singing life over me. The final picture is yet to be unveiled. The Master Artist covers the unfinished painting with His *pure white cloth*, keeping it from damage, revealing its beauty on that day. He is the Master Artist, so I say, "Paint on, Lord. Paint on."

"What was meant to stop me has actually served to advance the spread of the Good News." (Philippians 1:12)

"For I know (with confidence) that this will turn out for my deliverance and spiritual well-being, through your prayers and the (superabundant) supply of the Spirit of Jesus Christ (which upholds me)." (Philppians 1:19)

Lesson from Sweeping the Floors

The sweep, weep, seek of communion.

Skin in the Game: Incurred risk by being involved in achieving a goal.

I hoped to go to church today, but it's a big, disappointing no. I couldn't cope with clothing touching my blackened armpit or my burnt, blistered chest from the month of radiation treatments. It's okay. I needed some alone time. Larry has been so faithful, calm, and supportive, but I needed to be alone, even if just for a couple of hours.

Once I realized I couldn't go this morning, I decided to sweep, weep, and seek.

The house didn't need cleaning, but I did. I began to *sweep* the floors and *weep* to God. I began to *seek* and give Him thanks for helping me through this incredible time of pain and the unknown.

I wept for the pain of the past few months, the pain of today, and the process I still faced. I sought God's will for the days to come. I knew God had a plan greater than myself. I wanted to close the doors of the past surgery and the month of radiation. I was on the other side and knew I would heal. But first, I must submit to the time necessary to heal from such deep burns.

There was very little to sweep off the bathroom floor. I gathered what there was into the dustpan and eyed the dark blobs. What did I sweep up? Touching it carefully, I realized it was moist and could be rolled into a tiny ball.

I wasn't sure whether to laugh or cry. I chose to laugh. It was me. I was sweeping up burnt skin that dropped to the floor as I moved about with the broom. I looked into the bathroom mirror. Gross as it was, I realized that true healing had begun. I cooled down the burning pain with more radiation cream, then sat down to rest and seek God for more strength and direction.

The following days brought more burnt skin peeling away, revealing fresh, pink, healthy skin. It wasn't an easy process. On the contrary, it was quite painful. Yet, the lesson came. I had skin in the game. This journey cost me more than I can detail here. It cost me time, pain, sleep. It cost isolation, privacy, health, and independence.

But what I gained can't be measured either: Trust. Peace. Wisdom. Sympathy. Compassion. Empathy. Insight. And yes, skin.

Because I have skin in the game, I can speak into the lives of others facing cancer and the loss of hope in the time of struggle. My experience with cancer gives my words for those facing cancer a weight they otherwise lack. I didn't know anything compared to what I do now. It's not about disease knowledge. It's about understanding such a personal, individual journey.

When each of our sons was born, the greatest joy was touching their skin. Counting each finger and toe brought a wonderful sense of acknowledging the miracle of life. All three are grown now. Each strong man is now a dad who loves the touch of his children. I recently heard one of them recount the birth of his children, as if no one could understand the wonder of that moment. I feel the same.

I doubt my boys know that when I hug them, I still see them as my sweet little boys. I'm confident Mary felt the same about Jesus, touching His newborn skin on that first day when she carefully wrapped him with strips of cloth and placed him in a manger until the day she beheld His limp, bruised, and bloody body upon the cross.

Mary and Jesus had skin in the game.

"We saw Him with our very own eyes. We gazed upon Him and heard Him speak. Our hands actually touched Him, the One who was from the beginning." (I John 1:1)

"He lifted the loaf of bread, and after a prayer of thanksgiving, He gave each of His apostles a piece of bread, saying, 'This bread is My body, which is now being offered to you. Always eat it to remember Me.'" (Luke 22:19)

Perhaps today, in the privacy of your home, prepare communion for yourself and/or your family. It's personal. He loves you.

Lessons from the Gift of Hope

Joy to the world!

Hope: A feeling of expectation and desire for a certain thing to happen; a feeling of trust.

What time do the children in your home wake up on Christmas morning? Perhaps you recall your own childhood memories of those early Christmas mornings. What made for your best memories? Was it the gifts or the smell of food cooking, snowflakes flurrying in the sky, or the bright lights on the tree?

I recently asked my adult siblings their favorite gift they received as children. It was challenging for each to recall a certain gift, but they all warmly recalled the joy of being together with Mom and Dad. For us, it wasn't about any physical gifts. Christmas was about feeling secure knowing we were loved and cared for by each other.

Of course, as children, we were excited to see what secrets lay under the tree. Like the Christmas song, we found it hard to sleep at night.

Around three in the morning, we would start asking if it was time to get up, only to be told to go back to bed. We obeyed but not one eye closed as we repeated the request every thirty minutes. By five, our pleading was answered by smiling, sleepy-eyed parents. The waiting and trusting built our excitement. The heightened anticipation was due to the soft whispers and muffled laughs from our parents late on Christmas Eve night. We heard footsteps and boxes bumping as Mom and Dad placed gifts under the tree.

Our gifts weren't wrapped. Each sibling's gifts were separately bundled together. I don't know how we knew which stack was whose, but we did. The living room door was kept closed as we dressed for the event. There were no matching pajamas, but we also didn't come as we were. We didn't have much, but we put on our best clothes, washed our tired faces, and combed our hair to enter the room for which we had long awaited.

Our hearts and minds were eager to make a mad dash into the living room, but that wasn't how it happened. Instead, we lined up from youngest to oldest. It was the only time being the second born of seven wasn't to my benefit. I'm sure most people thought we received very little, but I never saw it that way. There weren't stockings filled with gifts but empty cardboard candy boxes that Dad secured from the drugstore to hold our favorite fruits, candies, and nuts.

Soon as we got these treats, we took them to our bedrooms and spread our stashes on our beds, gleefully counting each item. It was the best feeling to have a banana, an orange, a tangerine, a couple pieces of ribbon candy, a candybar, and pecans from my grandparents' tree. Each child got one, maybe two, gifts.

It was worth every second of hope in the morning. Why? Because that hope provided and continues to provide expectation and trust. My six siblings and I can tell you without hesitation we were never disappointed. As we became parents and grandparents, we realized the gifts under the tree didn't give us hope. The love of parents who taught us to wait patiently and to be truly grateful gave us hope. Best of all, what we found wasn't under the tree but beautifully wrapped in our hearts.

Waiting refines our character, and mature character leads us back to hope. This kind of hope is not a disappointing fleeting gift, but the endless treasure of God's cascading love ever growing in our hearts.

Romans 8: 25 explains that hope means we must trust and wait for what is still unseen. "For why would we need to hope for something we already have?" Like the wise men hoping to one day see the Morning Star rise, our hope is set on what is yet to be seen. We wait patiently for the day of fulfillment when we, too, will see the Morning Star in the east.

My dear friend, continue eagerly waiting for your hope to be fully revealed by His return. As we celebrate Advent, remember it is not only about preparing for the Christmas season, but also—and even more so—for the season of His return. In the waiting, trust and hope are wrapped securely as a gift to you.

Meditate on or write down your favorite Christmas memory and what is being developed in you as you await His return.

Lessons from Mary's Song

All is calm, all is bright.

Favor: Overly generous act of kindness beyond what is due or usual.

Public humiliation was the least of Mary's fears as Gabriel announced God's great favor upon her. Having an angel appear would be fearful in itself, but God's generous act of kindness could cost Mary her life. To be pregnant before marrying Joseph was no small social mishap. She could be disowned by her family and publicly shunned or put away by her fiance. There was also a high probability of being stoned to death.

Mary was frightened by the angel's appearance and the announcement of her impending pregnancy. Confusion was heightened by who this child was to be: Jesus, Son of the Most High. Mary's only question was how this could be. Gabriel's response was quick: This child would be conceived by the overshadowing of the Holy Spirit. Mary's simple response was, "I am the Lord's lowly servant, and I am willing to accept whatever He wants. May everything you have said come true."

No wonder Mary was chosen!

I don't know about you, but I'd have at least ten more questions before the angel could get in another word. However, Mary's response is humbling.

A few days later, Mary visited Elizabeth, the soon-to-be mother of John the Baptist. At their meeting, Mary praised God with her new song "The Magnificent: Mary's Song of Praise."

I encourage you to read the song in its entirety in Luke 1:46–55.

A few highlights:

- Mary proclaimed God as her Savior.
- She stood in awe that God knows her by name.
- She honored and gave thanks for all His blessings upon her.
- Mary recognized God's mighty power over all Earth's inhabitants.
- Her spiritual hunger was satisfied in Him.
- She rested in the assurance of His faithful promises of mercy.

In our most frightening moments, God's presence changes chaos into calm and shines brightly eliminating dark places. What moments are you facing that may cause fear?

May we also respond with the heart of a humble servant, willing to accept God's great favor with a song of praise.

Lessons from Angels and Shepherds

It came upon a midnight clear.

Radiant: Glowing brightly; emanating or sending out a sweet aroma; emotional expressions such as joy, love, and good health.

How do you picture the night sky when the angel appeared to the shepherds announcing the birth of Jesus? Christmas cards and timeless carols create a cold, clear midnight sky with a zillion brightly shining stars scattered like diamonds across a velvety black background. Regardless of the weather, that night sky was ablaze in a split second. It glowed with the sweet aroma of the good news of joy, love, and peace on Earth. It was radiant.

That was obviously a busy season for Gabriel, who brought the good news to Mary and Joseph of the coming Messiah, Jesus. Gabriel also told Zechariah that his wife, Elizabeth, would give birth to John the Baptist.

Gabriel, the messenger angel, listens intently for the voice of the Commander to come, go, and announce. The name of the angel sent for this awesome announcement is not given. I think it's safe to suggest that Gabriel once again got the commission to proclaim this world-changing news!

It wasn't until preparing for this devotional that I realized there was only one angel who appeared to the shepherds. This angel reassured them that fear had no place here in the presence of the most joyous news the world ever heard, news for everyone everywhere. But boy, once that proclamation was made, the sky exploded with the brilliant light of a vast host of angels filling the sky above the shepherds and their sheep.

Of course, the stars weren't the focus or the source of the radiant beam casting cascading light across the field where the shepherds kept their watch. Perhaps even the sheep stood in awe as their Creator was glorified in the highest!

The shepherds weren't just doing a job. They kept guard among the sheep at night to stay close by. As they did, they did more than just care for the sheep. They fed, watched over, and stood guard around the sheep. They put themselves in harm's way to protect the flock. During the dark hours, wild animals and robbers would try to isolate a lamb to take it captive. Later, Jesus declared, "I am the Good Shepherd who lays down his life as a sacrifice for His sheep."

The night of Jesus's birth, the shepherds' response was joyous praise. They hurried to find the baby wrapped in cloth lying in a feeding trough. They didn't keep this news to themselves. They recounted to everyone who would listen what happened. They praised God and glorified him for all they had heard and seen, just like the angels did.

Emmanuel, God is with us! Let us proclaim it to everyone everywhere! Jesus Christ is born!

Lessons from Star Gazing

The thrill of hope.

Ecstatic: The removal of the mind or body from its normal place of function; delirious, fervent, overjoyed, beside oneself with happiness.

Have you ever found hope in an unexpected place? The wise men, filled with hope, searched the night sky for the promised star, a prophetic promise yet unseen. Just like us, in times of uncertainty, they clung to a ray of hope to guide them. This hope, fueled by the desire to see His star, that rising Morning Star, did not rely on what they felt or saw but was based on the Prophetic Word.

Imagine gazing into the night sky with them, as Numbers 24:17 whispers a promise: "I see Him; but not now; I behold him, but not near. A scepter (a symbol of the king) shall rise out of Israel."

Think of a moment in your life when a long-awaited hope turned to joy. Can you feel the surge of excitement that filled the wise men when the star rose? This wasn't just any star. It defied the natural order, moving south from Jerusalem to Bethlehem, a path stars don't normally take. Its unique light must have felt like the fire by night that guided their forefathers, a tangible presence of hope and guidance.

Oh, that level of joy! But what about when the star disappeared from view? Did joy wane? Was their hope deflated? Consider how, like them, we often continue in faith even when the signs are no longer clear. The wise men continued in the direction where they last saw His star. Upon first seeing it, they bowed in worship. When they found the star over the home of

100

Joseph and Mary, their response was the same.

What about us? When we face times of uncertainty, can we—like them—stay the course and worship?

On your journey, when your guiding star seems to vanish, stay the course and worship until it reappears. Just as the wise men did, hold onto the promise of His return. We will witness the Morning Star rise again from the east, a symbol of a new dawn and enduring hope.

2 Peter 1:19 reflects on this enduring promise: "For this prophetic message is like a piercing light shining in a gloomy place until the dawning of a new day, when the Morning Star rises in your hearts."

Matthew 2:10 captures their unrestrained joy: "And when they saw the star, they were overwhelmed and so excited that they shouted and celebrated with unrestrained joy."

In moments of doubt or darkness, hold onto this promise. Like the wise men, our joy will be uncontainable when we witness His glorious return. Just as they did, we will celebrate, filled with joy and hope, when we see Him coming in the clouds of glory!